Bee Careful

Good

Be

appy

A gift for

From

weet

Bee

Good

ind

Bee Careful

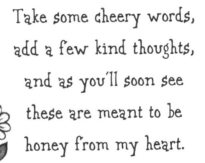

Take some cheery words,
add a few kind thoughts,
and as you'll soon see
these are meant to be
honey from my heart.

Honey from My Heart
for You

Honey

Bee Happy

Illustrated by Debra Jordan Bryan

Published by J Countryman
A division of Thomas Nelson, Inc.,
Nashville, Tennessee 37214

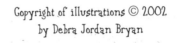

Project Editor—Terri Gibbs

Designed by Left Coast Design, Portland, Oregon

ISBN: 0-8499-9530-2

www.jcountryman.com
www.thomasnelson.com

Printed in China

You're the kind of person
I'm so glad to know,
someone who
fills life's little corners
with a sunny glow.

While bees make sweet honey
they smile at each day,
and be it rainy or sunny,
they cheerfully say,
"Today is the BEARY
best day of the year!"

I thank God
upon every
remembrance of you.

Philippians 1:3

Bee Good

Tomorrow's assignment:

_____

_____

_____

_____

_____

Bee Kind

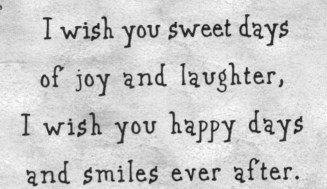

I wish you sweet days
of joy and laughter,
I wish you happy days
and smiles ever after.

Some other things I wish for you:

_____

_____

_____

_____

The bees make
golden honey,
and you make
life sunny!

Can you count the honey bees,
in the sky so blue?
Nor can you count the ways
our Heavenly Father
cares for you.

Happiness is
like honey, . . .

it's more fun
when shared.

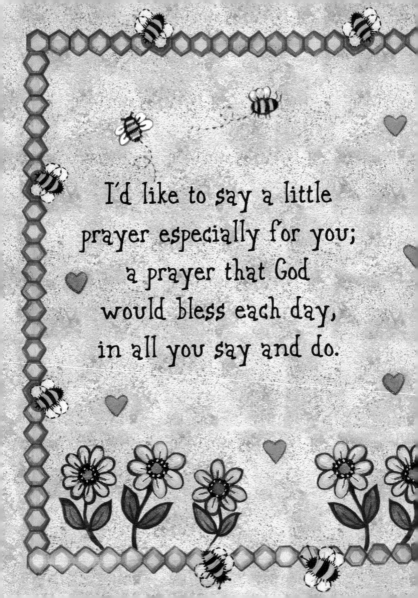

I'd like to say a little
prayer especially for you;
a prayer that God
would bless each day,
in all you say and do.

A little prayer for you:

_____

_____

_____

_____

_____

Someone to share
someone to care,
someone to say,
"You'll be okay,"

. . . that is honey
for the heart!

I hope that you've enjoyed
this honey from my heart—
a short but
sincere way to say, . . .

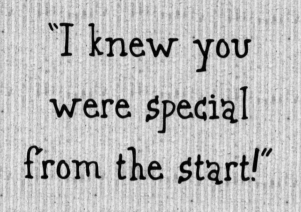

"I knew you
were special
from the start!"

Bee Sweet  Bee Kind

Bee Happy  B

Bee Kind  Bee Careful

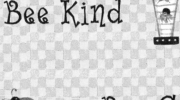 Bee Good  Bee

Bee Careful 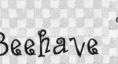 Beehave

 Bee Sweet  Be